MOTHER IS BLESSED

A Sermon And
Order Of Service
For Mother's Day

BY ROBERT J. CAMPBELL

C.S.S. Publishing Co., Inc.
Lima, Ohio

MOTHER IS BLESSED

9322 / ISBN 1-55673-602-9

To my mother, Lawilda Elizabeth Campbell, whose life implanted in me, and whose memory continues to nurture, the Holy Spirit's gift of patience.

Table Of Contents

Introduction   7

Order Of Service   9

Hymn   14
For All Mothers Everywhere

Sermon   17
Memories Of Mother

Introduction

"Necessity is the mother of invention," the old truism goes. Certainly it is true of this dramatic monologue, "Memories Of Mother." I wrote it for Mother's Day, 1992, in an attempt to offer something more than the usual platitudes connected with this day.

I began to think of how the nurturing of mothers is back of much of the greatness and goodness in people, and then of how Paul's mother might have impacted on Paul. The dramatic monologue provided the necessary form for expressing the creative spirit I had in mind. I could remain true to the historical data on Paul as much as it is available, and yet exercise what one seminary professor called a "sanctified imagination" to read between the lines and make educated guesses as to how one event links to another in the apostle's life. As I connected in this way to Paul's life, I found myself also connecting to my own memories of my mother, and to my sense of who I am. This, in turn, helped to flesh out the imagining.

I began to hear it in my mind as Paul ruminating around the creation of his letter to the Corinthian Church, and I focused on 1 Corinthians 13 as the heart of his reply.

I staged it in a contemporary way that was comfortable for me, with a small table and wastebasket near the front pews. I found the nearness helped establish a sense of intimacy with the congregation, and facilitated the use of their imagination for what followed. Remembering and thinking aloud, I paced around the table. The pacing also helped the congregation use their imagination and created intimacy with "Paul." I tossed crumpled paper into the wastebasket as I began, and wrote furiously at the table at the end.

This setting worked for me. Others might want to establish one that is more authentically first century, with costume for Paul, and perhaps a scroll in place of notebook paper. The scene could also be depicted with Paul dictating to his scribe.

I would anticipate the use of this piece by pastors for the Sunday celebration of Mother's Day. It could also be used for a program at mother-daughter banquets or other celebrations of Mother's Day. In the latter case, especially, it could be adapted so that a woman stands in the background and plays the part of Paul's mother, or that a woman's voice came through the speaker to do the same.

Order Of Service

GATHERING

Organ Prelude

Welcome

Introit

*Call To Worship

Leader: According to an old Jewish saying, "God could not be everywhere, and therefore he made mothers."

People: That is exaggeration, but in exaggeration there is truth.

Leader: The truth is, God does enfold us through the arms of our parents.

People: And the further truth is, God calls us in the congregation to be not only sisters and brothers to each other, but mothers and fathers to the little ones in our care. For by our baptism we are made one family.

Leader: In this worship let us recall the gift of God's presence through the mothers in our midst and the mothers in our memories.

Hymn: "Now Thank We All Our God"

LISTENING

Children's Moments

*Act Of Praise: Jesus' Mother's Song — Luke 1:46-55

Leader: My soul doth magnify the Lord,

People: **and my spirit hath rejoiced in God my Savior.**

Leader: For he hath regarded

People: **the lowliness of his handmaiden.**

Leader: For behold, from henceforth

People: **all generations shall call me blessed.**

Leader: For he that is mighty hath magnified me;

People: **and holy is his name.**

Leader: And his mercy is on them that fear him

People: **throughout all generations.**

Leader: He hath showed strength with his arm;

People: **he hath scattered the proud in the imagination of their hearts.**

Leader: He hath put down the mighty from their seat,

People: **and hath exalted the humble and meek.**

Leader: He hath filled the hungry with good things;

People: **and the rich he hath sent empty away.**

Leader: He remembering his mercy hath helped his servant Israel;

People: **as he promised to our forefathers, Abraham and his seed, for ever.**

*Gloria Patri

Sharing Concerns

Pastoral Prayer

The Lord's Prayer

Scripture: 1 Corinthians 13

Anthem

Sermon: "Memories Of Mother" — a dramatic monologue based on the apostle Paul writing to the church at Corinth.

RESPONDING

Hymn: "Faith Of Our Mothers" — from "Faith Of Our Fathers, and substituting "mothers" for "fathers."

Litany For Mothers (author unknown)

Reader 1: O Lord, help all mothers in the divine task of mothering.

Reader 2: Help them to see their children's problems through their eyes.

Reader 1: Keep ever before them their own childhood so that they will not expect too much.

Reader 2: Give them the patience of the silent stars; give them a sense of humor.

Reader 1: Help them to win their children through love instead of compelling them through fear.

Reader 2: Help them to teach their children that every home is an altar and that every wish is a prayer.

Reader 1: Help the mothers today to face their doubts and skepticism, and to rise above them.

Reader 2: Help them radiate faith in the basic goodness of life.

Reader 1: Give them back strong hands for guidance when youth falters and would turn back.

Reader 2: Help them to teach their children to live bravely and to meet defeat courageously.

Reader 1: Help them to teach their children that real character is what we are alone with ourselves in the dark.

Reader 2: Help them to teach their children that the value of their lives will be measured by the service they give.

Reader 1: Help them to teach their children that true happiness is not found in things, but in the unfolding of their minds and souls.

Reader 2: Help the mothers today to make their lives go on in their children's — but bigger, finer, nobler than they ever dared to be. Amen.

Offering

Offertory, Presentation of Gifts

*Doxology, Prayer of Dedication

*Hymn "For All Mothers Everywhere" by Robert J. Campbell (to the tune of "For The Beauty Of The Earth" by Dix)

*Postlude

*Indicates the congregation stands.

Other Possible Hymns

"Love Divine, All Loves Excelling" by Charles Wesley

"For The Beauty Of The Earth" by Folliot S. Pierpoint

"Joyful, Joyful, We Adore Thee" by Henry Van Dyke

"O Lord, May Church And Home Combine" by Carlton C. Buck

"Happy The Home When God Is There" by Henry Ware, Jr.

"Where Charity And Love Prevail" Translated from ninth century Latin by Omer Westendorf

"Help Us Accept Each Other" by Fred Kaan

"Our Parent, By Whose Name" by F. Bland Tucker

"When Love Is Found" by Brian Wren

For All Mothers Everywhere

By Robert J. Campbell
To the tune of "For The Beauty Of
The Earth," (Dix)

1. For all mothers everywhere,
   for God's love brought down to earth,
   for the joy divine, they share
   in the miracle of birth.
   > Refrain: Lord of all, to You we raise
   > this our song of grateful praise!

2. For our mother's loving arms,
   first to lift us in this life,
   strength and nerve in life's alarms,
   hands that heal in hurt or strife.
   > Refrain: Lord of all, to You we raise
   > this our song of grateful praise.

3. For our mother's listening ears,
   for her presence always there,
   in our laughter, joy and tears,
   and her willingness to share.
   > Refrain: Lord of all, to You we raise
   > this our song of grateful praise!

4. For our mother's cherished voice
   singing songs that pacify,
   speaking truth in time of choice,
   consolation when we cry.
   > Refrain: Lord of all, to You we raise
   > this our song of grateful praise!

5. For the mothers who have died,
   gone from us to be in heaven,
   for the memories that abide,
   and eternal presence given.
   > Refrain: Lord of all, to You we raise
   > this our song of grateful praise!

6. For all living mothers, too,
   for the love of Christ they live,
   for the strength they find in you,
   and ability to give.
   > Refrain: Lord of all, to You we raise
   > this our song of grateful praise.

7. For the mothers yet to be,
   for the future children, too,
   for love shared unendingly,
   and unending trust in You.
   > Refrain: Lord of all, to You we raise
   > this our song of grateful praise!

8. For all mothers everywhere
   hope of all for love's rebirth,
   and the vision of their prayer
   for a family of earth.
   > Refrain: Lord of all, to You we raise
   > this our song of grateful praise!

Memories Of Mother

The Apostle Paul Broods About His Contrary Children
(A Mother's Day Sermon Based On 1 Corinthians)

O, for goodness' sakes, what am I going to write to this church of mine? Church? No, it's more than a church. This is my family. These are my children! Yes, I gave birth to this family of faith at Corinth.

For so long I'd been a failure. Those hotheads at Lystra, they stoned me. The intellectuals at Athens, they snubbed me and laughed at my belief in the resurrection! Then I came to this most unpromising of cities, its streets overrun with prostitutes and thieves, and criminals and shady characters of all sorts. Then, to my surprise, they responded to the gospel of God's love. They kept coming back to hear more about Jesus. We built a family of faith there, brothers and sisters celebrating his resurrection from the dead!

Then I had to leave my baby, and go on to preach Christ in other towns and cities. But Corinth is my family; these are my children!

But they're sure spoiled rotten! How childish their behavior has been! All this fighting and bickering, and hormones out of control! I thought Apollos would help them grow up. He's such a gifted preacher! But they made him the eye of a hurricane! Now some follow Apollos, and some Peter and some Paul. Some, in their smugness, say I follow Christ! As if nobody else did! Goodness gracious! All this fighting.

And all these middle age people who think they're teenagers discovering sex for the first time, unmarried people living together, married people going after others' husbands and wives, men having sex with men and women with women, and now these latest reports that've come to me, cases of prostitution and even incest at Corinth! Goodness gracious. I expect this in the world. But these are my "new born" in Christ. These are his children, and mine! O how do I help them grow up?

I need to be a mother, but I'm a man. The seminary didn't train me to mother people. My favorite teacher, Gamaliel, stressed the manly virtue of fighting for God. My other teachers drilled me in debate. And that's the sort of thing I'm good at. By nature, I love a fight. Sometimes I provoke people just to get their attention. They may throw stones. But at least they don't go to sleep! I'm a soldier for Christ, always combat ready. But how can I combat these divisions without being combative? How do I get my children to make peace, and find their soul's peace in God?

I really do need to be a mother. I wonder . . . what would my mother have done?

It's been so long since she passed away. I miss her. She was such a help back when I was a child, back when I had not given up "childish ways."

Ah, yes, that brings back a memory of a thing that few of my Christian friends know about. I'm a grownup now, and they think I've always been. They think I've always been this mature dedicated soldier for Jesus. But I was a real trouble-maker when I was a kid. I was real mixed up, a real loner who got in lots of trouble. From day one I was crazy on religion. It drew me like a magnet. I wanted God to rule the world. I wanted everybody to think like I thought about it. And the other kids made fun of me. But I was no wimp. I was a fighter. I was small, but strong as an ox.

One day I took on a kid twice my size, and threw him to the ground. He got a fist in my eye, but I pounded his head into the ground, and I would have killed him, except my mother pulled me off! She took me and shook me and then she held me, and spoke softly: "God has better ways, my son! Two wrongs don't make a right, Saul. Be patient with people, like our Father in heaven has been patient with us. These other kids, son, don't be too hard on them. They want the God you've got. They're just too afraid to admit it. It's not cool in their crowd, son. And they think, if they lose their crowd, they will lose all they've got, and they'll be all alone. Listen to me, son. And don't return evil for evil. But hold your

18

head high, and go about God's business, and someday they're going to want to know about your God.''

My mother counseled patience, not only with other people, but with myself. For more than once, I was ready to give up and go with the crowd. I could fight only so long, then I'd think, "Why fight it? Nobody's going to be different! There's always going to be rioting in the streets, beatings, brutality and bloodshed. Nations will always go to war to try to get the upper hand. And the hand of the mighty is always going to crush the hand of the weak. In my worst moments I'd say, "Why, if Messiah ever does come, most likely it will end in a riot and more bloodshed. And afterwards, people will go on just like they did before.''

When I thought this way, I not only got the blues, I got into a black mood of despair. It was a thorn in my flesh, that I asked God to take away. But God would never do it. God's only answer was: "My grace is sufficient for thee.''

There was just one person who could draw me out of these moods; through her came the sufficient grace of God. Oh, how I miss her grace on days like this. For she believed in me even when I couldn't believe in myself, even when I thought God no longer believed in me. I miss her arms, and the look in her eyes. And though I didn't appreciate it then, I miss her motherly advice. For when those black moods hit, she would sit me down in front of a piece of my favorite cake and say, "Saul, you've got to remember, faith is more than a feeling, and God is more than a mood! You can't live your life, son, based on what others think. For then it wouldn't be your life, it would be theirs! You've got to believe the sun still shines when it's blacked out by clouds, and you've got to believe that God believes in you, even though you don't see it. Hang onto God through the darkness, and go the way you and he have worked out, no matter what anybody else thinks. You've got just one shot at it here on earth. Make it your life, son, not theirs!''

My mother's belief in patience came out of her study of the scriptures. I guess everybody kind of picks out his favorite scriptures, and in that way makes up his own Bible. Well, my mother picked out the ones that had to do with patience. One day she called me outdoors after a storm and pointed to a rainbow stretching from one end of the horizon to the other. She told me, "Just once in thousands of years, God lost his temper, and wiped out all families but one with a flood. But that was the only time, and when it was done, he set a rainbow in the sky as a sign that he would never lose his patience again!"

She remembered lots of stories, my mother did. But she never read them. She told them anew in her own words, as we sat round in a circle. And some times she recited the poetry of scripture, especially about the "mercy of God" being "from everlasting to everlasting."

There was one part of the Bible she loved more than the stories and poetry. She drew most of all from the promises of God, especially the promise of the Messiah. Messiah would deliver Israel, and set us free from hated Roman control. Messiah would also be God's light for the world, and God's peace for the soul, and between neighbors and nations. Messiah would come, that was the hope that sustained her when a Roman sword went through my brothers's heart after he and others had caused a riot in the streets of Jerusalem.

My father scoffed at her dream. Messiah was a fairy tale, made up by men who were not men, by men who lacked the backbone to fight for their freedom. If Israel wants deliverance, he'd say, Israel had better not wait on God. Israel had better begin to store up arms!

My mother would just smile at these remarks. She would say, "Be patient son. Don't give up hope. A thousand years are but a day in God's sight. Wait on the Lord. Messiah's coming. I feel it in my bones. The time is near. Maybe in your lifetime, Saul. Be ready, son. Don't miss him if he comes; I want you to greet him for me!"

Well, I almost did miss him. For I didn't realize he'd come as "a man of sorrows," acquainted with grief. I didn't know he would show his love by, of all things, dying for us. Nor did I have any idea a man could actually rise from the dead, and have power to make his loving Spirit live in us again and again and again!

But, praise God, Messiah was patient like my mother, and as I set out to arrest his followers, he arrested me with his forgiveness, and convicted me of sin, and then pardoned and released me from the prison of my prejudice! O, if only my mother could have lived long enough to see this day!

Strange, though, my mother's love was so like my Savior's, that, maybe in a sense she did know him, and he, her. For he spent his life telling us to judge not lest we be judged, and to love everybody without exception, and lay down our lives if we have to, to love others like he loved us. And on the cross, he loved his enemies like he told us to do, and prayed for them, "Father, forgive them, they know not what they do."

Before mother's spirit left and her heatbeat and breathing stopped, her last words were: "Be patient, my son, above all be patient. Never give up on love son, never, never, never. God is love, son, so love is all God has to give, because that's all God is. Love is God's gift, Saul, so if you lose love, you've lost everything and then, you are nothing. Never give up loving yourself or others or God. Be patient, Saul, for love is the only wealth that is forever and ever. People are childish, Saul, always fighting for things that don't last, things your spirit can't take with you when your body goes to the grave. They fight over their inheritance, son. But money is not forever and ever. They fight over who knows more, and who can best see into the future. But knowledge is imperfect, son, like the image of your face in a mirror fogged over by moisture. And knowledge passes away, like your face does when you step back from the mirror. These things aren't real, son. Love is real. For ever and ever love is real."

Well, enough of this reminiscing! I've still got to write my children. But maybe now I know what I have to say. I'll always be a man and not a mother, but as long as my mother's spirit lives in my memory, I'll have power to help my contrary children. I'll have a nurturing in me to share with them.

So, to these children at Corinth, playing their childish games of who follows the greater preacher, and who has the greatest spiritual gift; to these middle-aged teenagers trying to outlust each other with the greatest sex drive, this is what I'll write:

"If I speak in the tongues of men and of angels, but have not love, I am a noisy gong or a clanging cymbal. And if I have prophetic powers and understand all mysteries and all knowledge, and if I have all faith, so as to remove mountains, but have not love, I am nothing.

"If I give away all I have, and if I deliver my body to be burned, but have not love, I gain nothing.

"Love is patient and kind; love is not jealous or boastful; it is not arrogant or rude.

"Love does not insist on its own way; it is not irritable or resentful; it does not rejoice at wrong, but rejoices in the right.

"Love bears all things, believes all things, hopes all things, endures all things.

"Love never ends; as for prophecies, they will pass away; as for tongues, they will cease; as for knowledge, it will pass away. For our knowledge is imperfect, and our prophecy is imperfect; but when the perfect comes, the imperfect will pass away.

"When I was a child, I spoke like a child, I thought like a child, I reasoned like a child; when I became a man I gave up childish ways. For now we see in a mirror dimly, but then face to face.

"Now I know in part; then I shall understand fully, even as I have been fully understood. So faith, hope, love abide, these three; but the greatest of these is love."